About this book

MW01691287

The Language Bear's dual-language books are self-directed learning tools and are specifically designed to help young children better understand foreign words and phrases. The teaching methods used in this book allow children to learn at their own pace and enjoy the learning process. These methods include:

Repeat words

Numbers

Simple phrases

Highlighted words

Contextual vocabulary

Corresponding imagery

Bosley Sees the World

Join Bosley Bear on his first adventure outside the cave when he discovers how big the world is and how much there is to explore.
He learns about trees, birds, rocks, mountains, rivers and so much more, teaching your child as he learns.

Find Bosley Sees the World and more dual-language books at:
www.theLanguageBear.com

Dedicated to my
wife and two boys
who inspire me to be
a better person everyday.

Bosley Goes to the Beach

ISBN-13: 978-1484880791
ISBN-10: 148488079X

The Language Bear Bilingual Books
207-370-4298
info@theLanguageBear.com
www.theLanguageBear.com

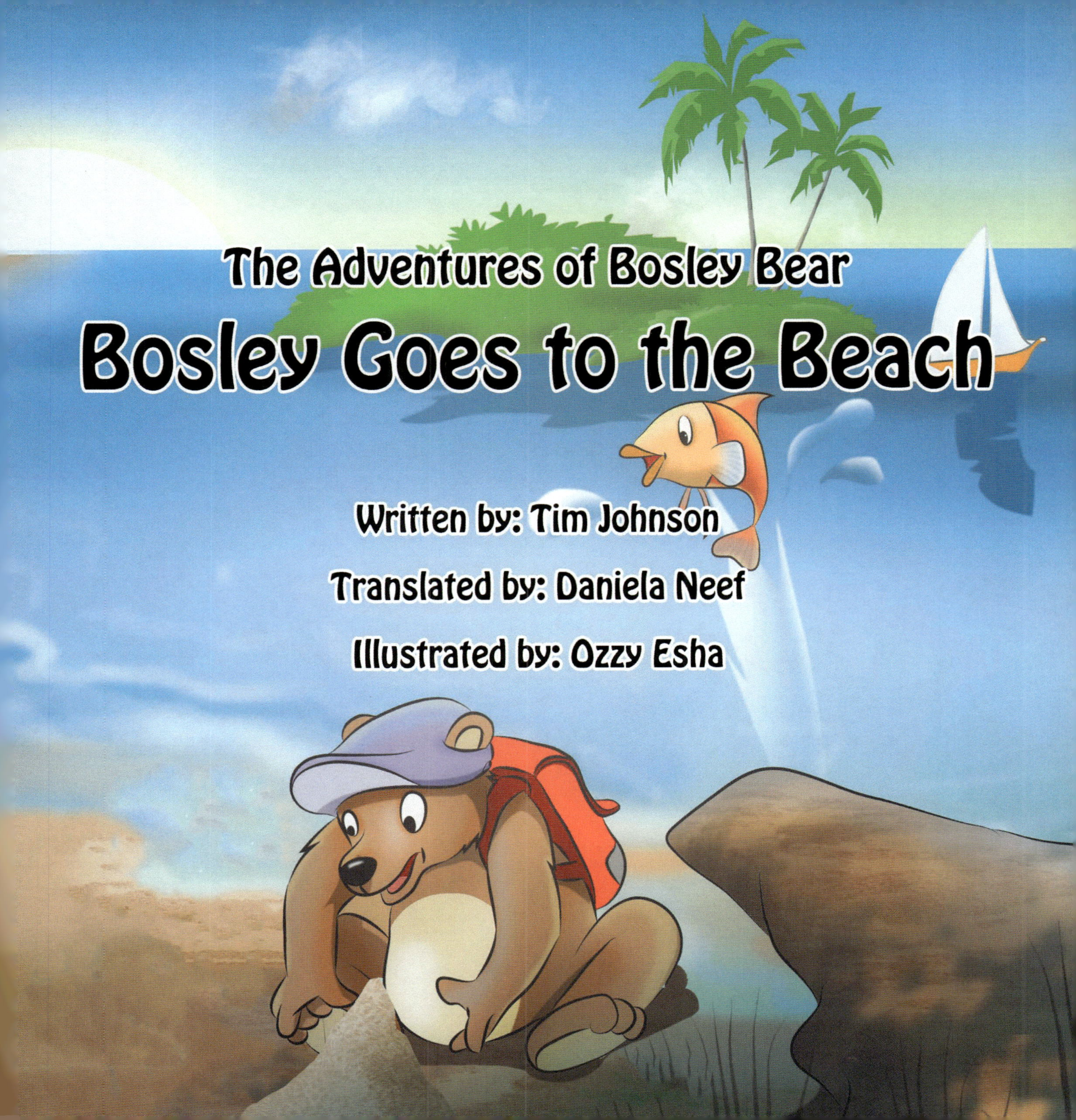

The Adventures of Bosley Bear

Bosley Goes to the Beach

Written by: Tim Johnson

Translated by: Daniela Neef

Illustrated by: Ozzy Esha

It was morning and Bosley knew today would be a great adventure.

He looked out the window.

It was going to be a beautiful day.

Es war Morgen und Bosley wusste, dass heute ein großartiges Abenteuer sein würde.

Er sah aus dem Fenster.

Es würde ein schöner Tag werden.

He packed his toys into a big red bag.

He packed big toys, and little toys.

Er packte seine Spielsachen in eine große, rote Tasche.

Er packte großes Spielzeug ein, und er packte kleines Spielzeug ein.

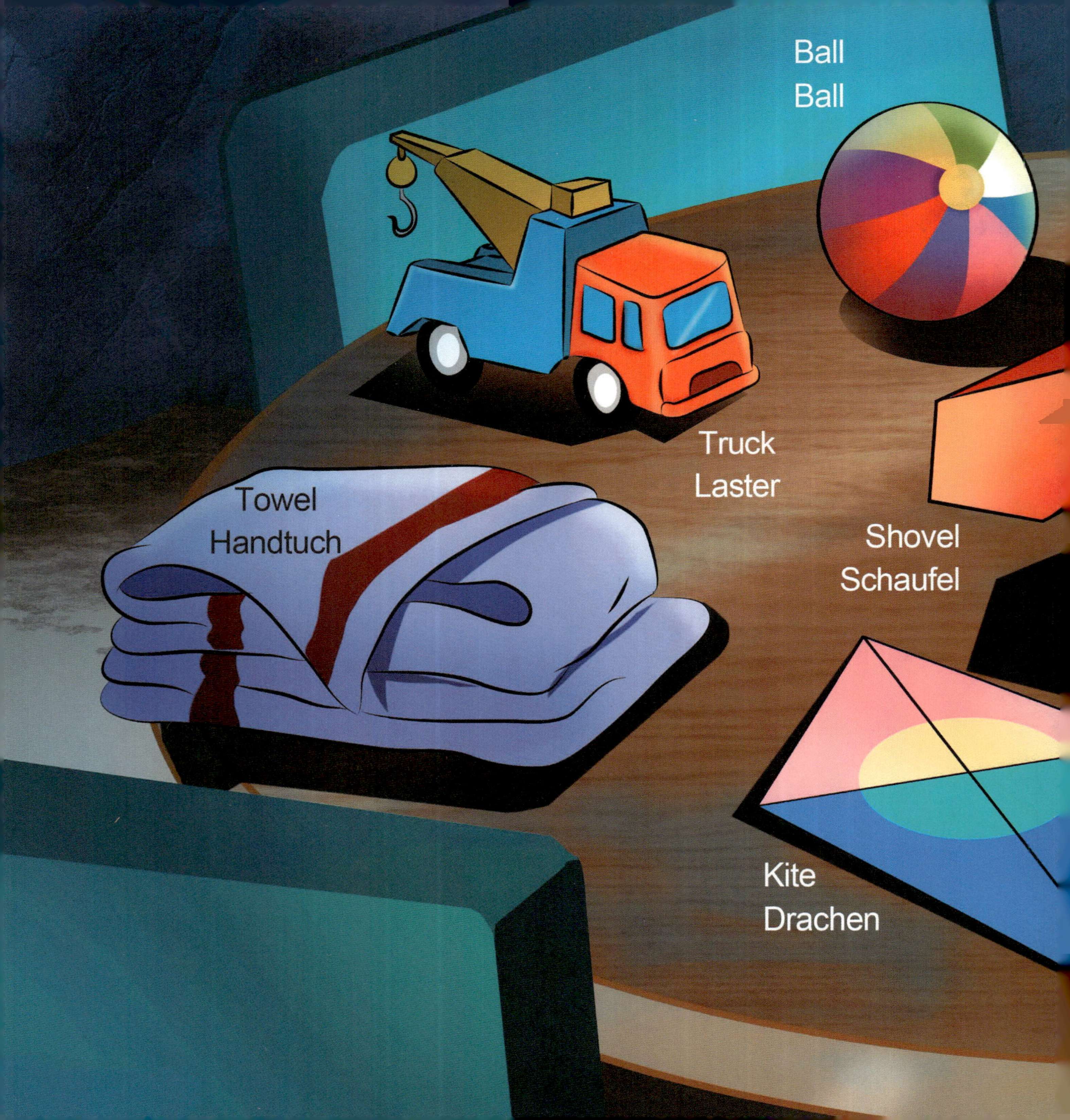
Ball
Ball
Truck
Laster
Towel
Handtuch
Shovel
Schaufel
Kite
Drachen

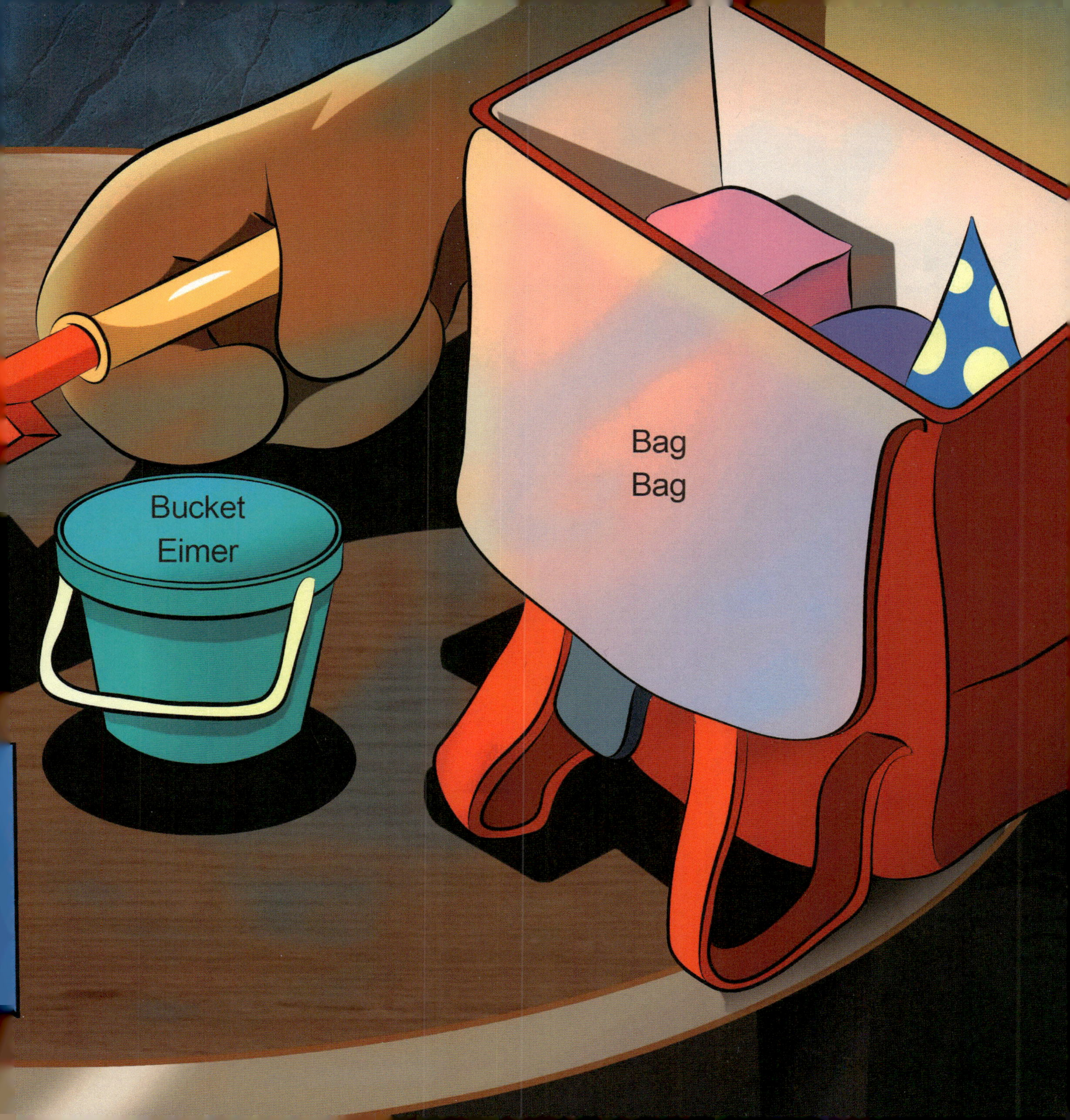
Bucket
Eimer
Bag
Bag

Bosley had everything he needed for a day at the beach.

"Mama, I'm ready to go!" he announced.

"Alright, let's go!" Mama said.

Bosley hatte alles, was er für einen Tag am Strand brauchte.

„Mama, wir können gehen!", verkündete er.

„Okay, lass uns gehen", sagte Mama.

When they arrived at the beach, Bosley stopped and looked around.

It was so big. He had never seen the sea before.

There were so many new things to explore.

Als sie am Strand ankamen, blieb Bosley stehen und sah sich um.

Es war so groß. Er hatte noch nie das Meer gesehen.

Es gab so viele neue Dinge zu entdecken.

Bird
Vogel
Sun
Sonne
Sand
Sand
Crab
Krebs
Seashell
Muschel

Clouds
Wolken
Island
Insel
Sailboat
Segelboot
Fish
Fisch
Rocks
Felsen

Bosley put down his big red bag and ran through the sand.

He ran through the water and jumped into the waves.

Bosley legte seine große, rote Tasche hin und rannte durch den Sand.

Er rannte durch das Wasser und sprang in die Wellen.

A fish jumped out of the water and yelled to Bosley.

“Welcome to my home!” the fish called out.

“You live in the ocean?” asked Bosley.

“Yes I do,” answered the fish.

“What a wonderful place to live,” Bosley thought.

"I wish I could swim like a fish.”

Ein Fisch sprang aus dem Wasser und rief Bosley

„Willkommen in meinem Zuhause!“, rief der Fisch.

„Du lebst im Meer?“, fragte Bosley.

„Ja das tue ich“, antwortete der Fisch.

„Was für ein wunderbarer Ort zum Leben“, dachte Bosley.

„Ich wünschte, ich könnte schwimmen wie ein Fisch.“

A bird flew over Bosley's head.

"This is my home up here," squawked the bird.

"That looks like an exciting place to live," replied Bosley.

"I wish I could fly like a bird."

Ein Vogel flog über Bosleys Kopf.

„Das ist mein Zuhause hier oben", krächzte der Vogel.

„Das sieht nach einem aufregenden Platz zum Leben aus", antwortete Bosley.

„Ich wünschte, ich könnte fliegen wie ein Vogel."

Bosley walked through the shallow water and heard a small voice saying,

"Welcome to my home." He looked around and saw a small crab next to him.

"Did you say that?" asked Bosley.

"Yes," replied the crab. "I live in the shallow water. I protect myself with my sharp claws."

"Those are nice claws," exclaimed Bosley. "I wish I had sharp claws like you."

Bosley was very happy to meet new friends, but he was ready to play with his toys in the sand.

Bosley lief durch das flache Wasser und hörte eine leise Stimme sagen,

„ Willkommen in meinem Zuhause." Er schaute sich um und sah einen kleinen Krebs neben sich.

„Hast du das gesagt?", fragte Bosley.

„Ja", antwortete der Krebs. „Ich lebe im flachen Wasser. Ich schütze mich mit meinen scharfen Scheren."

„Das sind schöne Scheren", rief Bosley. „Ich wünschte, ich hätte so scharfe Scheren wie du."

Bosley was sehr glücklich, neue Freunde zu treffen, aber er war bereit, um mit seinem Spielzeug im Sand zu spielen.

He opened the big red bag and took out a bucket to build a sand castle.

He made one pile of sand.
He made two piles of sand.
He made three piles of sand.
He made four piles of sand.

He added four walls, a tiny door, and four small twigs as flags.

He was very proud of his sand castle.

Er öffnete die große rote Tasche und holte einen Eimer heraus, um eine Sandburg zu bauen.

Er machte einen Sandhaufen.
Er machte zwei Sandhaufen.
Er machte drei Sandhaufen.
Er machte vier Sandhaufen.

Er fügte vier Wände, eine winzige Tür und vier kleine Zweige als Fahnen hinzu.

Er war sehr stolz auf seine Sandburg.

Bosley called out to the fish.

“Hey fish, do you like my sand castle?"

"Yes I do," replied the fish. "I wouldn't be able to do that, I only have these fins”.

Bosley rief den Fisch.

„He Fisch, magst du meine Sandburg?”

„Ja das tue ich“, antwortete der Fisch. „Ich könnte das nicht machen, ich habe nur diese Flossen“.

Bosley asked the bird, "What do you think of my sand castle?"

"It's beautiful," said the bird. "I can't do that with my wings."

Bosley fragte den Vogel, „Was hältst du von meiner Sandburg?“

„Sie ist wunderschön“, sagte der Vogel. „Ich kann das mit meinen Flügeln nicht machen.“

Bosley asked the crab, "What do you think of my sand castle, crab?"

The crab was very impressed. "I would only make a hole in that bucket with my sharp claws."

Bosley realized that he could do something that none of the other animals could do.

He realized that his paws were very useful.

Bosley fragte den Krebs, „Was hältst du von meiner Sandburg, Krebs?“

Der Krebs war sehr beeindruckt. „Ich würde mit meinen scharfen Scheren nur ein Loch in den Eimer machen.“

Bosley erkannte, dass er etwas tun konnte, dass keines der anderen Tiere tun konnte.

Er erkannte, dass seine Pfoten sehr nützlich waren.

"Mama, I can't swim like a fish, I can't fly like a bird, and I can't pinch like a crab, but look what I built!"

"What a beautiful sand castle."

Mama bear was so proud. "You're right Bosley, there are lots of things you can do that no one else can do."

Bosley began to think of all the other things he wanted to build and he had a very busy afternoon.

„Mama, ich kann nicht schwimmen wie ein Fisch, ich kann nicht fliegen wie ein Vogel, und ich kann nicht kneifen wie ein Krebs, aber schau, was ich gebaut habe!“

„Was für eine schöne Sandburg.“

Mama Bär war so stolz. „Du hast Recht Bosley, es gibt so viele Dinge, die du tun kannst, die niemand anderes kann.“

Bosley fing an, an all die anderen Dinge, die er bauen wollte, zu denken und war den ganzen Nachmittag beschäftigt.

Wall
Wand
Chair
Sessel

Tree
Baum
Mountain
Berge
Cave
Höhle
River
Fluss

When Bosley returned home from the beach, he was very tired.

After dinner he went right to bed.

He was eager to sleep because he knew tomorrow would be another great adventure.

Als Bosley vom Strand zurückkehrte, war er sehr müde.

Nach dem Abendessen ging er gleich ins Bett.

Er war schlafbegierig, weil er wusste, morgen würde er ein weiteres großartiges Abenteuer erleben.

The End

Ende

New words:	neue Wörter:
Morning	Morgen
Window	Fenster
Toy	Spielzeug
Big	groß
Little	klein
Beach	Strand
Ocean	Meer
Sand	Sand
Water	Wasser
Fish	Fisch
Swim	schwimmen
Bird	Vogel
Fly	fliegen
Welcome	willkommen
Crab	Krebs
Friends	Freunde
Fins	Flossen
Wings	Flügel
Sharp	scharf
Busy	beschäftigt
Tired	müde
Bed	Bett
Tomorrow	morgen

25135493R20025

Made in the USA
Charleston, SC
16 December 2013